The
Successful Celebrant

Developing A Positive Mindset

Build a creative, inspiring, happy,
prosperous and life-enhancing
celebrant practice

By Veronika Sophia Robinson

The Successful Celebrant
© Veronika Sophia Robinson
Published by Starflower Press for:
Heart-led Ceremonies Celebrant Training
Published March 2023
ISBN 978-1-7393353-7-3

Though short and simple, the contents of this book have the power to change your life. It is written on the assertion that by creating new thought patterns, and combining mindset and heart recalibration, you will create a successful celebrant practice, and indeed, life.

Veronika Sophia Robinson has been a professional celebrant since 1995, and alongside her husband, Paul, has been a trainer at Heart-led Ceremonies Celebrant Training since 2017. Veronika is a metaphysician, and has long understood the power of the mind to shape our reality. She has previously worked with hypnotherapist, Brian Head, in New Zealand, leading sessions in self-hypnosis for elite sportspeople; and has facilitated metaphysics workshops for Unity School of Metaphysics in Auckland.

She lives in rural Cumbria, England, where she has a thriving, healthy and enjoyable celebrant practice. Veronika is the author of many books including Write That Eulogy: the art and craft of biographical storytelling; Wedding Celebrant Ceremony Planner; and Funeral Celebrant Ceremony Planner.

Many years ago, I had the pleasure of working with Brian Head, a hypnotherapist in Auckland, New Zealand, facilitating self-hypnosis sessions for elite sportspeople. These people were the best in their field, competing nationally and internationally. Despite, or even because of, their skill and talent, they knew that to keep competing at the top level their mindset had to be laser sharp and focussed. Our sessions were based on planting success messages into their subconscious so that they would then be expressed in their external world. The work I did with those people can be applied to your role as a celebrant. It is about speaking, writing, envisioning and feeling your success, and committing to this process every single day.

YOU, and you alone, are responsible for your success as a celebrant, not a funeral director or a wedding planner or other celebrants or even your celebrant trainer.

It doesn't matter how many directories we're featured on, or how many funeral director doors we knock on, or how we build our celebrant wardrobe, or our skill set with public speaking or writing scripts, or the jazzy way we promote ourselves on social media, our most important asset is our mindset and heart story.

This book may appear simple, but it has the power to change your life. It is written on the assertion that by creating new thought patterns through positive, life-affirming and success-oriented affirmations, you will create a successful celebrant practice. They are based on my work with elite sportspeople and my daily envisioning as a celebrant. I know they work.

Many people come into this profession with the idea that most of our work involves standing before an audience. As you know, it is a small part of our work.

Everything we do leads to that point, it is true, but much of what we do is invisible to others. And so too is it with our mindset. No one would argue that most of our work as a celebrant is 'unseen'. While our mindset is also unseen, the manifestations of those thoughts are highly visible.

We can wear designer clothes, have a swish website, and effective branding, awesome styled photo shoots, but if inside we don't believe in ourselves then the externals will soon become less effective. *The Successful Celebrant* has been written to show how, with as little as five minutes a day, you can change how you think and feel, and therefore change your whole celebrant practice.

The best way to work with affirmations, in my experience, is by writing them down *every single day*, preferably TWICE a day. What we're doing is 'brainwashing' ourselves with new thought patterns until we truly believe them, and that to think anything else is incomprehensible.

The Power of Now
One key point is that affirmations must be written in the present moment. They need to be said as if you already have the object of your desire or stated intention. For example, you wouldn't write or say "I am going to be a successful celebrant" because "going to be" puts it in the future or out of reach, if you like. If you say "I am a successful celebrant" you give it, and yourself, immediate authority. It carries a sense of power. You are the owner of that belief and thought form, and it has no choice but to materialise in your world.

Embody The Energy
However, generally it's not enough to just say or write your words. For an affirmation to work it has to be a marriage between your *thoughts* and your *feelings*. It is a co-creation of the two. You can write

6

"I am a successful celebrant" a thousand times but the day you FEEL that you're a successful celebrant is the day your business will change forever. *Engaging with your emotions* allows you to embody the energy of that which you desire. It raises your frequency, which causes shifts in Universal Energy. Yes, you're that powerful! You have the ability to be a powerful manifestor.

The reason for this is simple: there are more connections going from the heart to the brain than there are from the brain to the heart. Our heart, where our feeling self emanates from, is quite literally at the heart of creating a beautiful life.

What I'm advocating in this simple book WORKS! I routinely see in my own practice that I attract the most incredible couples, from all walks of life and from around the world, for beautiful and meaningful ceremonies. They find me easily and effortlessly, and are keen to work with me. I wish this for you too. I also see it in the other ceremonies I officiate, too, and how there are amazing synchronicities between me and my client and/or the former life of the deceased.

The Right Time To Write
The affirmations chosen for this book can be adapted to suit your own desires and needs, if preferred, and as prompts or can be used as is. I recommend that you write down the ones you particularly want to focus on (or all of them), every morning. Ideally, first thing before you engage in social media, conversations with those you may live with, news, and even coffee. When we first wake we're in a place of being more readily able to accept new information. Make the most of this liminal time to re-educate yourself.

Writing them just before sleep ensures you take these ideas with you into your dream state.

Through my years of practising affirmations, which I've been doing all my adult life, I've become so used to it that I default to them whenever I have nothing else going on in my head. For example, when I'm driving, sometimes I don't put music on. Instead, I just enjoy feeding my mind positive affirmations. It's fun, it's empowering, and I've seen it create miracles in all aspects of my life. Ready to start?

How Do I Make These Work?
There are two ways that I tend to work with affirmations. One is to simply write it as it is: e.g. "I am a successful celebrant". The other is to preface it with gratitude: "I am SO grateful that I'm a successful celebrant". Regardless of which version you use, infuse it with *feeling*. Feeling is key. It might be hard to imagine at first. ACT AS IF. Act as if you truly are a successful celebrant, and let that wonderful feeling permeate your whole being.

When I'm practising gratitude, I allow the feeling of joy and appreciation to fill my heart, and then I imagine that feeling going through my whole body. And then, it carries on filling the room, stretching outside my home, and into the fields and beyond the hills, beyond the county, and right across the country, the world, and to the farthest reaches of the Universe. *When you're feeling that level of gratitude, everything changes!*

If you've ever been to the gym or undertaken any sport or regular exercise, or learnt a musical instrument or other skill, you know that you have to be committed and disciplined if you expect to see results. It's no different at all with changing your mindset and vibration.

As with anything where we want to become an expert, it takes about 10,000 hours of practice. Our mind is such a powerful tool, and it is there to work for us. Consider your feelings as the fuel in your manifestation engine, and the brain as the key in the ignition. You need both to take off along the road of becoming a master manifestor.

Consciously Creating Your Reality
You might wonder why you'd bother writing affirmations such as "I am a compassionate celebrant" or "I am a gentle celebrant". They might seem obvious to you. Think of them as keeping you on track, or even as course correction if you're feeling jaded or overworked.

From Dormant to Dominant
As we seek to create new neural pathways, and fire them up with the fuel of vibrant and genuine gratitude, we go from dormant to dominant thoughts. Your dominant thought and feeling is what you'll attract into your life. It's the foundation practice of the Law of Attraction.

Investing in Yourself

By taking the time each day (preferably twice a day) to consciously create your dream celebrant practice, you are investing in yourself. The process of writing and feeling your affirmations, when done correctly, will elicit true joy, and it will be a part of the day you really look forward to. It's dedicated time for internal harmony, and the idea of skipping it will soon become non-negotiable. To be clear, this is a life-long practice, not something you do for a week or month and then stop. The world is constantly bombarding us with information. Our job is to CHOOSE which thoughts we'll entertain on a minute-by-minute, hourly, and daily basis.

I've divided the affirmations to reflect the different aspects of our life as a celebrant. You might prefer to focus on one area at a time, or work on enhancing, amplifying or changing every area at the same time. There's no right or wrong. All that's required is a genuine desire to create the celebrant life of your dreams.

You will need:
- Quiet, uninterrupted time.
- Allow at least five minutes morning and night. If you can devote 15 minutes to half an hour to each session, even better. You'll see results in no time. You might be thinking "I don't have half an hour to write out affirmations!" I lead a busy, active and fulfilling life. Writing my affirmations is integral to that life. It can be tucked in quite easily, such as while you're having a cup of tea, or before you get out of bed in the morning. Your mindset is the most powerful resource you have, not just as a celebrant, but in all aspects of your life. Being guardian of the thoughts you think and the way you feel is your superpower, if you let it be.
- Notebook
- Pen

As you approach an affirmation, recognise that it is a powerful tool to transform your life.

Allow it to stand alone. Breathe it in. Understand what it means for you.

Retraining your mind is not a process to be rushed but rather like a gentle walk in a Zen garden. Take your time. Honour the changes as they begin to take place within you.

You have the power to change yourself, and therefore the power to change the world, one beautiful thought and feeling at a time.

The Power of I AM
Any time you start a sentence with I AM you are creating what and who you are and what/who you want to be. The words we choose after "I am" should be positive. We are quite literally identifying ourselves with the words which come

after them. For example, in my daily life rather than say "I am so tired!"I would reframe it to "I am ready to sleep."

Some of the affirmations which follow start with I AM. Others start in a different way. Each of them can be rewritten or spoken to commence with I AM if preferred. They can be written and spoken with the addition of the words "I am so grateful that..." before each one. I find by adding those words it allows me to really enter into the feeling of gratitude.

My Body

Our body is the home we consistently live in throughout our whole life. It's an abode we often take for granted. Yes, we bathe, dress and perhaps preen in front of the mirror, but how many of us are truly aware of our body and the way we move and express ourselves within it?

These affirmations will allow you to bring awareness to this part of your life. The more at ease and comfortable we are in our body, the more at ease we will be in front of other people.

"The game of life is a game of boomerangs.
Our thoughts, deeds and words
return to us sooner or later
with astounding accuracy."
~ Florence Scovel Shinn

I am so grateful that...

I live, move and have my being
with grace.

I move with confidence.

My body is an enjoyable place to live.

My mannerisms are pleasant,
graceful and welcoming.

I have an engaging presence.

I am relaxed and calm.

The calmness of my being allows others
to feel at ease in my presence.

My superpower is exuding calm.

My body is radiantly healthy,
fit and energetic.
This enables me to live fully and freely.

I live, move and have my being
in confidence.

I joyfully eat nourishing foods
and drink nutritious beverages
to energise and enhance my wellbeing.

I am a wonderful example
of what it means to be at
home in one's skin.

The more confident I am in my body
the more confident I am
in putting myself out into the world.

I lovingly take care of my body,
and enjoy dressing and adorning myself.

Alignment

To live in alignment means that we consistently show up as a person who lives their values, speaks with truth, and acts from integrity. From this foundation, we create balance between mind, body and soul. This internal harmony ensures that we are vibrating at a frequency which matches our higher, authentic or best self rather than ego or adhering to societal influences. The beauty of living this way is that it nurtures and consistently guides us.

As a celebrant, our alignment means that we are in agreement with our values: the thoughts, choices and direction we seek in our practice. This internal harmony guarantees we shall have more joy in our life.

I am so grateful that...

I am naturally aligned.

I am seeing everyone's magnificence.

I am always in the right place,
at the right time,
and with the right people.

Just by being me,
I attract golden opportunities.

I control the world around me
by my perception.

I live by my values,
and attract others into my world
who mirror what I hold dear.

My values are my guiding light.

By living my truth, I inspire others.

Creativity

*"If I am not actively creating something,
then chances are I am probably
actively destroying something:
myself, a relationship,
or my own peace of mind."*
~ Elizabeth Gilbert, author of *Big Magic*

I am so grateful that...

I am allowing my
imagination and ideas to create.

I generate ideas easily.

I have the ability to bring new things
into existence.

I allow myself to be exploratory
in thought and action.

I allow my life to be transformed.

I am original, imaginative,
and flexible.

I transform
ideas and imagination
into reality.

I am curious.

I am playful.

I am open-minded.

I am a risk-taker with
my skills and talents.

I am intuitive.

I am flexible.

I am putting energy into my work.

I am passionate about my tasks.

I am enthusiastic.

Creativity is at the heart of my life.

I love to play, create,
invent and imagine.

Creating comes easily to me.

I allow my deepest inspirations
to be a creative force within.

It is safe for me to share
my creativity with the world.

My clients are overjoyed
with my creativity.

My creative flair makes
the world a better place.

My creativity brings delight to others.

My creativity is a healing balm.

As I create, I heal myself and others.

To create is to live with purpose.

Living On Purpose

To live on purpose means that you choose how you feel, how you think, and what you do.

In order to do this, it is crucial that we understand what is meaningful to us, what we're passion about, what we wish to put into the world, and how we view ourselves and others.

This motivation to live with passion, inspiration, direction and clarity means that we see our life through a long-pan lens and in close-up.

I am so grateful that...

I am a happy celebrant.

I am a joyful celebrant.

I am a grateful celebrant.

I am harmonious celebrant.

I am a graceful celebrant.

I am a gentle celebrant.

I am a giving celebrant.

I am a competent celebrant.

I am a successful celebrant.

I am a serene celebrant.

I am well-rested,
nurtured and nourished.

I take care of myself, and prioritise
relaxation, pleasure and fun.

I am always learning.

I choose to grow
personally and professionally.

I make time to nourish my inner self.

I love to bring beauty into this world.

I live and act with
integrity and kindness.

I am known for
my attention and care to detail.

I take professional pride
in every aspect of my celebrant business.

The more beauty, compassion and joy
I bring into my life,
the more I have to share with others.

Naturally Gifted

Each of has something we're naturally gifted in or at, that sets us apart from others because we do that particular thing well. It comes easily to us. Perhaps we are gifted in many ways. It's easy to take these gifts for granted. To be clear, a gift is something that we have a natural talent for and isn't something that we've learnt whereas a skill is something we can become good at through consistent practice.

It could be that your gifts are ones that may have been ridiculed when you were a child, and so you 'tucked' it away. One such example is empathy. Oftentimes empaths are told they are 'too soft' or 'too sensitive'. Empathy is a true gift, for it allows us to feel our oneness with everyone on the planet.

I am so grateful that...

My natural gifts are
welcomed in the world.

My ceremony clients are drawn
to my innate gifts.

I readily share my qualities with others.

My natural gifts
are what make me unique.

I allow my intuition to guide me
personally and professionally.

My intuitive voice
is always accessible to me.

I listen to my inner wisdom
to find just the right words.

As I hold the space for others,
I create a safe and welcoming
energetic embrace.

My empathy ensures others feel heard.
When they feel heard, they start to heal.

I allow myself to be in tune
with other people's feelings.

Compassion comes easily to me.

I am kind and caring.

My gifts are safe to share with others.

I honour my natural talents.

My talents were bestowed upon me
for a good reason.

I combine my natural gifts with my
well-developed skills to create
wonderful ceremonies.

My gifts and qualities
are integral to being of service.

The Path of Success

To accomplish our aims or goals as a celebrant means we have succeeded. It is important to think of our celebrant practice as a journey rather than a specific destination point. Crucial to this is recognising that each celebrant has their own definition of what success means. For some, it might be about the number of ceremonies they officiate each week. For another celebrant, it might be measured on the quality of the ceremonies they create. And for another, success is measured by the relationship they have with their clients, and the ability to attract kindred spirits into their life. Regardless of how you measure it, the bottom line is that on your journey you seek to do your best, and that you have a balance between work, play, home, family and friends, creativity, abundance, good health, and boundaries, and celebrating yourself in the process.

I am so grateful that...

I am a successful celebrant.

I am an intuitive celebrant.

I am a creative celebrant.

I am a reliable celebrant.

I am an organised celebrant.

I am a professional celebrant.

I am a skilled celebrant.

I am a valued celebrant.

I am meeting my goals and aims.

I love my work as a celebrant.

I value my clients,
and other industry suppliers.

I create the work and life balance
that best suits me.

I welcome my ideal
ceremony clients now.

My celebrant practice is prosperous.

Every day in every way
I enjoy healthy and thriving celebrancy.

I am a wonderful community celebrant.

My celebrant success
is measured in ways
which are unique to me and my needs
and desires.

I am an inclusive celebrant.

I unravel my biases and prejudices,
and welcome people into my world
with ease and heart.

My People

Although I am an inclusive celebrant, and welcome clients from all walks of life, belief systems, and ways of living, I also honour how much I truly enjoy working with kindred spirit or soul-friend or soul-mate clients. There is a wonderful inner transformation when we attract such people because it reflects that we live our lives on purpose. Any celebrant who has ever experienced a difficult client, archetypal bridezilla or groomzilla will understand the difference it makes, personally and professionally, to work with dream clients. Any celebrant can create this for themselves by lighting an internal fire which glows and attracts others to their inner hearth. It's both magical and magnetic. This soulful way of living and being will make you an irresistible magnet, and you'll enjoy your work even more.

I am so grateful that...

I am attracting wonderful new clients.

I work with
like-minded individuals,
couples and families.

I serve families
from all walks of life.

I am easily attracting people
who value my qualities and skills.

I am a client magnet.

I attract
soul-friend clients.

People love to work with me.

My clients feel supported
when they work with me.

My clients feel valued and understood
when they work with me.

I love how good it feels when
me and my clients are on the same page.

My values are a beacon to
kindred-spirit clients.

My clients feel valued, held,
supported and appreciated
when they work with me.

It is so easy for me to be found by
wonderful people who are keen to
have me as their celebrant.

Like attracts like,
and so I put out the energy
I wish to see mirrored.

I only attract loving, kind,
warm-hearted, open-minded
and generous people into my world
for they are a mirror of who I am.

Ceremonial Work

It is in every celebrant's interests to ask themselves this question every day:
"What do I want to put out into the world?"
The answer to this serves as a beacon in the way we live, move and have our being. It keeps us conscious of our purpose.

"The Law of Attraction states that whatever you focus on, think about, read about, and talk about intensely, you're going to attract more of into your life."
~ Jack Canfield

I am so grateful that...

I create personalised ceremonies.

I create beautiful ceremonies.

I create meaningful ceremonies.

I create ceremonies
which heal people.

I create ceremonies
which truly reflect my clients.

My ceremonies
change people's lives.

Ceremony creation comes easily to me.

I welcome my ceremonial inspiration
and readily share this with my clients.

I bring all my gifts, qualities and skills
to ceremony creation with ease,
confidence and clarity.

Rituals

Rituals are like pictures in a storybook. That is, they augment the narrative.

While a ceremony is the overarching service we officiate, rituals are moments within the ceremony that are based on carefully choreographed actions attached to specific symbolism.

I am so grateful that...

I create rituals the world
has never seen before.

I respect time-honoured rituals
with awareness for tradition,
familiarity and comfort.

I administer to the sacred task
of ritual creation
with awareness, intuition and care.

I write rituals with understanding
of the connection between
mind, body and soul.

I choreograph rituals
with beauty and grace.

The rituals in my ceremonies
paint pictures.

My ceremonial rituals are
powerful and meaningful.

Communication

To be a celebrant is to be a professional in communications. The ceremony is where we bring it all together: our listening, intuition, writing, speaking, and performance.

I am so grateful that...

I am an excellent listener.

I listen without agenda or judgement.

I listen without interruption.

I listen as I seek to understand.

I am comfortable with silence.

Listening allows me to connect deeply.

I listen to my intuition,
and trust the guidance I receive.

Listening is a gift I give to my clients.

As I listen, I know they feel heard.

I am a creative writer.

My writing is organised.

I write with flair.

My words illuminate the page.

With each drop of ink,
I am making the world a better, kinder,
more beautiful place.

I am a disciplined writer.

I am a wonderful writer.

I am a brilliant ceremony-script writer.

Writing comes to me easily.

Ideas come to me faster than I can write, and they're all fabulous ideas.

I am a powerful writer.

I write with clarity, consciousness and creativity.

I write with ease and flow, and edit with attention to detail and clarity.

Every day I am developing my writing skills.

My writing provides an excellent foundation for my ceremonies.

My clients love the words I write.

I write words which reflect what is meaningful to my clients.

I have a strong voice.

I am eloquent.

I speak clearly.

My diction is excellent.

I have a powerful yet gentle voice.

My voice is a joy to listen to.

I am aware of the landscape
of my vocal range.

I am familiar with how my voice works.

I have a beautiful speaking voice.

My voice is attractive to all who hear it,
myself included.

My voice engages, comforts and
encourages people.

My voice amplifies
the wonderful words I've written.

I speak with passion and purpose.

Every day I work on vocal exercises to
keep my vocal indentity
strong, vibrant and healthy.

I am a confident public speaker.

I perform with ease.

I am comfortable in front of an audience
no matter the size.

I present in a natural way.

I am filled with calm and confidence
as I officiate my ceremonies.

I navigate my ceremony script with flair.

I am mindful of my mannerisms.

Organisation

I am so grateful that...

I am organised.

I am a competent celebrant.

My paperwork and administration
are in order.

I deliver ceremony scripts on time.

I keep accurate notes and files
on all my clients and ceremonies.

When I make a promise to a client,
I deliver.

I work efficiently.

I am punctual.

My Place

I am so grateful that...

I am creating a beautiful body of work.

People love to work with me.

I leave a legacy of incredible ceremonies.

I am creating an inspiring, wonderful
and engaging online presence.

My professional pride
ensures a wonderful reputation.

I love being of service.

I make the world a better place
simply by being me.

My work is love made visible.

It is safe for me to be visible.

Right Livelihood

We have been indoctrinated with the false belief that 'money is the root of all evil.' This is not true. Money amplifies who we are.

I am so grateful that...

I have a
successful and enjoyable career
as a celebrant.

I love what I do and I do what I love.

I earn at least .....a month,
doing ceremony work I love
and that is easy for me.

It is a joy to receive income
which honours the
wonderful work and energy
I put out into the world.

I am paid well for being of service.

I am grateful for the enjoyable exchange
between me and my clients.

I love to work with and for my clients,
and they love to honour my work
by paying me well.

People love to work with me,
and they love to pay me.

I love to earn, spend, share,
save and invest money.

Money is unlimited.

Good people do good things
with money. I am a good person.

Cooperation

One of the most important things to understand as a celebrant is that no one can steal your clients. *What's meant for you will not pass you by.* Let go of comparing yourself to other celebrants.

I am so grateful that...

I enjoy being part of
a wonderful network of local celebrants.

We support and encourage each other.

I am grateful to work with
wonderful suppliers in my industry.

There is room for everyone's dreams.

I am always in the right place,
at the right time, with the right people.

Milton Keynes UK
Ingram Content Group UK Ltd.
UKHW022204040824
446478UK00004B/166